simple appetizers

simple appetizers

easy recipes for effortless entertaining

RYLAND
PETERS
& SMALL

LONDON NEW YORK

Recipe credits

Valerie Aikman-Smith
Gazpacho with smoked salted toasts
Parmesan wafers
Pretzel bites
Salt-crusted citrus shrimp with chili dipping sauce

Fiona Beckett
Cheese and basil soufflés
French onion soup
Pea and Parma ham crostini
Seared steak carpaccio with truffle vinaigrette and arugula

Maxine Clark
Cherry tomato, bocconcini, and basil salad on bruschetta
Parma ham with figs and balsamic dressing
Spicy crab in phyllo cups

Ross Dobson
Chickpea, tomato, and green bean minestrone
Chili salt squid
Naked ravioli with sage cream

Lydia France
Grilled lamb skewers with garlic and saffron sauce
Shrimp cocktail shots
Vermouth scallops with green olive tapenade

Tonia George
Crab bisque
Pea and smoked ham soup with mint

Louise Pickford
Fresh asparagus with hollandaise sauce

Jennie Shapter
Mini spring rolls with chili dipping sauce

Fiona Smith
Chicken liver pâté with blueberry and balsamic glaze
Classic Caesar salad
Double zucchini and Parmesan salad
Pickled salmon with fennel and cucumber
Pork and hazelnut rillettes with pickled cucumbers
Smoked mackerel and preserved lemon pâté
Smoked mushroom pâté

Laura Washburn
Apple, beet, and fennel salad with Roquefort

Photography Credits

Martin Brigdale
Pages 21, 40, 44
Peter Cassidy
Pages 4–5, 9, 34, 43, 47, 51, 56
Jean Cazals
pages 14, 17, 18
Lisa Cohen
page 6
Gus Filgate
endpapers, pages 2, 39
Jonathan Gregson
pages 13, 26, 29, 48
Richard Jung
pages 1, 25, 29, 59
William Lingwood
page 10
Diana Miller
pages 33, 37, 52
Yuki Sugiura
pages 22, 30
Ian Wallace
page 63
Kate Whitaker
pages 55, 60
Polly Wreford
page 3

Notes

• All spoon measurements are level unless otherwise specified.
• Eggs used in the recipes in this book are large unless specified otherwise.
• Ovens should be preheated to the specified temperatures. All ovens work slightly differently. We recommend using an oven thermometer and suggest you consult the maker's handbook for any special instructions, particularly if you are cooking in a fan-assisted oven, as you will need to adjust temperatures according to manufacturer's instructions.

First published in the United States in 2010 by Ryland Peters & Small, Inc.
519 Broadway, 5th Floor
New York, NY 10012
www.rylandpeters.com

Text © Valerie Aikman-Smith, Fiona Beckett, Maxine Clark, Ross Dobson, Lydia France, Tonia George, Louise Pickford, Jennie Shapter, Fiona Smith, Laura Washburn, and Ryland Peters & Small 2010
Design and photographs © Ryland Peters & Small 2010

10 9 8 7 6 5 4 3 2

Printed in China

Library of Congress Cataloging-in-Publication Data

Simple appetizers : easy recipes for effortless entertaining / [text, Fiona Beckett ... [et al.]].
   p. cm.
Includes index.
ISBN 978-1-84597-989-8
1. Appetizers. 2. Cookery, International. I. Beckett, Fiona.
TX740.S4697 2010
641.8'12–dc22

2009041868

Commissioning Editor Julia Charles
Production Controller Toby Marshall
Picture Researcher Emily Westlake
Art Director Leslie Harrington
Publishing Director Alison Starling

Indexer Hilary Bird

RPS CICO BOOKS For digital editions visit www.rylandpeters.com/apps.php

contents

the best start

When entertaining at home, whether you are hosting an informal meal or planning an impressive dinner for a special occasion, you'll want your meal to get off to the best start.

The first course you choose to serve is all important as it whets the appetite and hints at what is to follow. Here, in *Simple Appetizers*, you will find a perfect selection of easy-to-prepare yet delicious recipes for both small bites to serve with drinks and plated dishes. Using only the freshest of ingredients, many of the recipes have an international influence but some are more familiar favorites.

The book features a variety of dishes taken from the colorful cuisines of the Mediterranean, inspired by the exotic flavors of Morocco and the Middle East, or spiced up with exciting South East Asian ingredients. What unites all the recipes is that they are surprisingly quick and easy to prepare and guaranteed to impress your guests.

To take the stress out of entertaining, many of the dishes can also be made well ahead of time and simply finished off or reheated as necessary once you are ready to serve. What's more, you will find that some of the recipes can be adapted to make more substantial meals that can be enjoyed for lunch or as a light dinner.

In *Simple Appetizers* you'll find plenty of inspiration and something to suit all tastes and every style of occasion, enabling you to enjoy stress-free entertaining time and time again.

small bites

pea and parma ham crostini

2 cups fresh or frozen peas

2 scallions

⅓ cup finely grated Parmesan

1 tablespoon finely chopped fresh mint or dill

2 tablespoons fruity olive oil

freshly squeezed lemon juice, to taste

sea salt and freshly ground black pepper

5 oz. thinly sliced Parma ham or other air dried ham, torn or cut into strips

CIABATTA TOASTS

2 ready-to-bake ciabatta loaves

olive oil spray or 4–6 tablespoons light olive oil

MAKES 18 CROSTINI

New season peas are deliciously sweet and make a perfect topping for crispy crostini. Salty Parma ham creates a lovely contrast in flavor but for a meat-free version simply omit the ham and top with generous shavings of Parmesan.

Preheat the oven to 350°F.

Cut the ciabatta on the slant into fairly thin slices. Spray both sides with olive oil or pour the olive oil onto a baking sheet and dip the slices of ciabatta into it. Bake in the preheated oven for 15 minutes, turning the slices halfway through the cooking time. Repeat with any remaining ciabatta slices. Let cool. (These toasts can be made in advance and stored in an airtight container until you are ready to top them.)

Cook the peas in plenty of lighly salted boiling water for 2–3 minutes, until just tender. Drain under cold running water. Trim and cut the scallions in half lengthwise, then slice them very thinly.

Put the peas and onions in a food processor and pulse until you get a chunky spread. Add the pecorino and mint and pulse again, then stir in the olive oil. Season to taste with salt, pepper and lemon juice. Spread the mixture thickly on the ciabatta toasts and drape a piece of ham on top. Don't wait too long before serving as the toasts will become soggy.

mini spring rolls
with chili dipping sauce

2 tablespoons sunflower oil

2 medium carrots, cut into matchsticks

½ cup snow peas, cut into matchsticks

¾ cup shiitake mushrooms, chopped

1 inch fresh ginger, peeled and grated

1 small red chile, seeded and chopped

1 cup bean sprouts

2 scallions, thinly sliced

1 tablespoon light soy sauce

2 teaspoons all-purpose flour

8 x 8-inch square spring-roll wrappers

oil for deep-frying

a deep-fat fryer

CHILI DIPPING SAUCE

5 tablespoons sweet chili sauce

1 tablespoon light soy sauce

MAKES 16 ROLLS

Spring rolls are best served immediately after cooking, but to keep last-minute preparation minimal you can make the filling up to 24 hours ahead. Fill the spring roll wrappers about 1 hour before cooking, but keep them covered so they remain moist until cooked.

Heat the sunflower oil in a wok or frying pan and stir-fry the carrots, snow peas, mushrooms, and ginger for 1 minute. Add the chile, bean sprouts, and scallions and stir-fry for 1–2 minutes, or until the vegetables are tender-crisp. Remove from the heat, stir in the soy sauce and set aside to cool.

Next, make the chili dipping sauce. Mix together the sweet chili sauce and soy sauce in a small bowl and transfer to a serving dish.

In a small bowl, mix the flour with 1 tablespoon water to make a paste. Cut the spring-roll wrappers in half diagonally and place under a damp cloth to keep moist. Remove one at a time to fill.

Divide the filling into four and put a quarter of one batch on the long cut side of a wrapper, placing it along the center, slightly in from the edge. Fold over the side flaps. Brush a little flour paste on the pointed end of the wrapper and roll up towards the point, pressing the end to seal. Repeat with the remaining wrappers. Keep covered until ready to cook.

Fill a deep-fryer with oil to the manufacturer's recommended level. Heat the oil to 350°F and deep-fry the rolls in batches for 2–3 minutes, until crisp and golden. Drain on paper towels. Serve hot with the chili dipping sauce.

pretzel bites

1 cup warm water
2 tablespoons butter, at room temperature, cubed
3 teaspoons rapid-rise yeast (instant yeast)
1 teaspoon granulated sugar
2¾ cups all-purpose flour
4 teaspoons baking powder
sea salt flakes, for topping
American hot dog mustard, to serve (optional)

MAKES ABOUT 40 BITES

In a glass measuring pitcher, mix together the warm water, butter, yeast, and sugar. Stir until the butter has melted. Put the flour in a food processor. With the motor running, pour the liquid into the flour in a steady stream until all of it is incorporated and the dough forms a ball. Add a little extra flour if necessary. Put the dough on a floured work surface and knead for 2 minutes. Form into a ball and put in an oiled bowl. Cover with a kitchen towel and leave to prove in a warm place for 1 hour.

Preheat the oven to 425°F. Turn the dough out onto a floured work surface and roll into a 12 x 6 inch rectangle. Cut 1 inch strips of dough from the long side and cut these into 1 inch bite-size pieces.

Put 4 cups water in a non-stick wok or pan (do not use aluminium), add the baking powder and bring to a boil. Drop the dough pieces into the water for about 1 minute and remove with a slotted spoon onto non-stick baking sheets. They will puff up. Sprinkle with salt flakes and bake in the preheated oven for 10–15 minutes until brown on top. Serve with the mustard for dipping.

parmesan and sage wafers

These delicate lacy wafers are ideal with a glass of prosecco, or try them instead of croûtons on a Caesar salad (see page 34.)

1 cup grated Parmesan
1 tablespoon finely chopped fresh sage
coarsely ground black pepper
sea salt flakes, for topping

MAKES 14 WAFERS

Preheat the oven to 350°F.

Mix together the Parmesan and sage and season with black pepper.

Drop tablespoons of the mixture at 2-inch intervals on a non-stick baking sheet. Pat down the mounds with your fingers. Bake in the preheated oven for 5–6 minutes until the mixture is completely melted and the edges are turning golden brown. Keep an eye on them as they brown fast.

Remove the wafers from the oven and set aside for a few moments to firm up. They will be soft when they come out of the oven but will harden as they cool.

With a spatula, carefully remove the wafers and arrange them on a wire rack to cool completely. Once cooled, sprinkle with salt flakes. They can be stored in an airtight container for 2 days.

grilled lamb skewers
with garlic and saffron sauce

1 lb. lamb loin fillet, cut into 30 cubes

2 tablespoons olive oil

1 tablespoon finely chopped fresh oregano

freshly ground black pepper

GARLIC AND SAFFRON CUSTARD

1 stick butter (8 tablespoons)

8–10 garlic cloves, coarsely grated

½ teaspoon saffron fronds

2 cups heavy cream

finely grated peel and freshly squeezed juice of 1 small lemon

sea salt, to taste

30 small wooden skewers, each about 6 inches long, soaked in water for 30 minutes before use

MAKES 30

The wonderful garlic and saffron sauce has the consistency of a crème Anglaise, but doesn't actually contain eggs. If it becomes too thick, dilute with a little lemon juice or white wine. It makes the perfect accompaniment to the skewers.

Put the olive oil, oregano, and black pepper in a dish. Add the lamb cubes, cover and marinate for about 2 hours.

When you are ready to cook, preheat the broiler to medium.

Thread the lamb cubes onto the prepared wooden skewers and put them on a baking sheet, loosely covering the exposed parts of the sticks with a little foil to prevent them from scorching. Set aside.

To make the sauce, gently heat the butter, garlic, and saffron together in a large, heavy-based skillet. Add half the cream and simmer until the cream bubbles and thickens, then add the lemon juice and turn down the heat.

Cook the lamb skewers under the preheated broiler for 2–3 minutes on each side and keep warm until ready to serve.

Add the remaining cream, lemon peel, and a little salt to the saffron cream mixture and stir over low heat until you have a thick sauce. Pour into a bowl and serve warm with the lamb skewers.

shrimp cocktail shots

¾ cup sour cream

2 tablespoons tomato ketchup

2 teaspoons Manzanilla sherry

a small handful each of fresh tarragon leaves and fresh dill, chopped

1 teaspoon Spanish smoked paprika (pimentòn)

a pinch of celery salt

2 scallions, roughly chopped

14 oz. cooked and peeled jumbo shrimp (about 60), tails left on

1 tablespoon snipped fresh chives or a pinch of Spanish smoked paprika (pimentòn), to garnish

freshly ground black pepper

shot glasses
toothpicks

MAKES 30 SHOTS

These miniature shrimp cocktails are an updated version of a seventies classic. To make them eye-catching you will need small, sturdy shot glasses and good-looking toothpicks. If preferred, you can arrange a little finely shredded lettuce at the bottom of the glasses in place of the scallions.

To make the cocktail sauce, put the sour cream, ketchup, sherry, herbs, paprika, and celery salt in a small bowl. Mix with a fork or small whisk until well combined and smooth.

Spoon a little cocktail sauce into each shot glass and add a few chopped scallions. Add 2 shrimp to each shot glass and garnish with either a sprinkling of chives or a pinch of smoked paprika, as preferred. Grind over some black pepper, if liked.

Serve immediately with toothpicks for spearing the shrimp.

vermouth scallops
with green olive tapenade

1 lb. fresh scallops (30–40)

1 tablespoon dry vermouth

2 tablespoons olive oil

1 cured chorizo sausage (about 10 oz.)

sea salt and freshly ground black pepper

GREEN OLIVE TAPENADE

⅔ cup green olives, pitted

3 scallions, finely chopped

1 large garlic clove

2 tablespoons dry vermouth

1 tablespoon chopped fresh flat leaf parsley

½ teaspoon sea salt

a stovetop grill pan

toothpicks

MAKES 30–40

This is a substantial yet elegant bite and one that lovers of a classic Martini cocktail will enjoy; it's a great way to kick off a dinner party. The scallops can also be served on thick slices of cucumber; one large cucumber is sufficient for this quantity of scallops. Try the delicious olive tapenade simply served spread on Ciabatta Toasts (see page 8.)

Put the scallops in a large bowl with the 1 tablespoon dry vermouth, olive oil, and a pinch each of salt and black pepper. Cover and let sit for about 10 minutes.

Heat a stovetop grill pan over high heat until very hot and sear the scallops for 1 minute on each side. Do not move the scallops during cooking—they are very fragile and they may tear.

Put the olives, scallions, garlic, 2 tablespoons dry vermouth, and parsley in a food processor with ½ teaspoon salt and give it a few short sharp blasts until the tapenade mixture looks chopped but not too mushy. Slice the chorizo so you have a slice for each scallop (not too thinly as you want it to support the weight of the scallop.)

To assemble, spoon a little tapenade onto each chorizo slice, put a seared scallop on top and secure with a toothpick to serve.

spicy crab in phyllo cups

PHYLLO CUPS
9 sheets phyllo pastry
4 tablespoons butter, melted

SPICY CRAB FILLING
8 oz. canned white crab meat
in brine, drained

3 oz. canned water chestnuts,
drained and finely chopped

1 inch piece of fresh ginger,
peeled and cut into fine strips

2 scallions, trimmed and
thinly sliced

finely grated peel and juice
of 1 lime

1 garlic clove, crushed

½ fresh red chile, seeded and
finely chopped

2 teaspoons sesame oil

2 tablespoons chopped fresh
cilantro leaves

sea salt and freshly ground
black pepper

*3 mini muffin pans, 12 cups
each, brushed with melted butter*

MAKES ABOUT 36 CUPS

These delicate bites are as light as air, but packed with fresh Asian flavors. Use canned white crab meat from the Pacific for these—not only does it taste very good, but there is no shell or messy bits to deal with if catering for a large number of people. It is also much cheaper than fresh crabmeat.

Preheat the oven to 350°F.

Unroll the phyllo. Stack the sheets on top of each other, then score the top sheet into 12 squares. Cut down through all the layers, giving 108 squares. Pile into 2–3 stacks and keep beside you in a plastic bag.

To make a phyllo cup, take 3 squares of phyllo, brush each with melted butter and lay one on top of the other, so that the points make a star, and do not touch each other. Quickly but gently press into one of the cups of the prepared muffin pan, so the points of the phyllo shoot upwards like a handkerchief. Repeat with all the remaining phyllo until you have 36 cups.

Bake in the preheated oven for about 8–10 minutes until golden. Remove, let cool in the muffin pan, then carefully transfer to a tray.

Put the crab meat in a bowl and fluff up with a fork. Stir in the water chestnuts, ginger, and scallions. In a separate bowl, mix the lime peel and juice, crushed garlic, chile, and sesame oil, and season to taste. Mix this into the crab mixture (this can be done up to 4 hours in advance), then stir in the chopped cilantro.

Fill the phyllo cups with the crab mixture just before serving (they can go a little soggy if they are kept too long.)

soups

pea and smoked ham soup with mint

3 tablespoons olive oil, plus extra to serve

6 scallions, chopped

2 garlic cloves, sliced

7 oz. thick slices of smoked ham, cut into cubes

1 tablespoon chopped fresh mint leaves or 1 teaspoon dried mint

4 cups peas (defrosted or fresh)

4 cups hot chicken or vegetable stock

sea salt and freshly ground black pepper

SERVES 4

Frozen or fresh peas make a very satisfying sweet and savory base for a soup. If you are into podding your own peas from the garden, the results will be even better, but frozen peas pulled out of the freezer are just as good as a standby.

Heat the olive oil in a large saucepan set over low heat and add the scallions. Cook for 2–3 minutes, then add the garlic, ham, and half the mint and cook for a further 2 minutes, stirring. Stir in the peas and pour in the hot stock. Simmer for 2–3 minutes until the peas are tender.

Transfer a third of the soup to a blender and liquidize until completely smooth. Pour back into the soup and mix until amalgamated. Season with just a little sea salt (the ham will be quite salty already) and some freshly ground black pepper. Add the remaining mint and stir.

Divide the soup between 4 serving bowls and serve with a drizzle of olive oil and a fresh grinding of black pepper.

French onion soup

1 sourdough baguette
or other long rustic loaf

2 tablespoons olive oil

3 tablespoons unsalted butter

2–3 large mild onions (about
1½ lbs. in total), thinly sliced

½ teaspoon granulated sugar

½ teaspoon dried thyme

⅔ cup dry white wine

5 cups beef, chicken, or
vegetable stock

white wine vinegar, to taste
(optional)

4 oz. Gruyère (rind removed),
coarsely grated

sea salt and freshly ground
black pepper

SERVES 4

French onion soup is one of the classic bistro dishes, made luxuriant by its melting cheese and crisp bread topping. Like many simple recipes it needs really good ingredients. The critical thing to remember is to cook the onions long enough and to use a substantial, densely textured bread, preferably a couple of days old.

Preheat the oven to 350°F.

Cut the bread into slices about 1 inch thick and lay on a baking sheet. Bake in the preheated oven for 15–20 minutes or until crisp and lightly browned, then set aside. (You can do this ahead of time.)

Heat the oil in a large ovenproof casserole, add the butter and tip in the onions. Stir so that they're thoroughly coated with oil and cook over low/medium heat, stirring them occasionally, until they turn a rich, deep brown. This may take up to 40 minutes, depending on your onions. Add the sugar once they start to brown, and stir more regularly—you don't want to burn them. Once the onions are a good color, stir in the thyme and wine and leave it to bubble up and reduce by half. Add the stock, bring back to a boil, and simmer for about 20–25 minutes. Check the seasoning, adding salt and pepper to taste and a few drops of vinegar if you think it tastes too sweet. Preheat the broiler.

Ladle the soup into 4 individual heatproof bowls. Lay the slices of bread over the surface of the soup, pressing them down lightly. Scatter over the Gruyère and broil for 5–10 minutes until the cheese is bubbling. Serve immediately.

gazpacho
with smoked salted toasts

3 lbs. ripe tomatoes

1 garlic clove

1 small red onion

2 small (Persian) cucumbers

1 green bell pepper

1 Serrano chile (red or green)

¼ cup extra virgin olive oil

¼ cup Jerez sherry vinegar

sea salt flakes and cracked black pepper

fruity olive oil, to drizzle

chives, to garnish (optional)

SMOKED SALTED TOASTS

1 small baguette

1 garlic clove, finely chopped

¼ cup olive oil

1 tablespoon smoked sea salt

SERVES 4

Try making this refreshing summer soup with heirloom tomatoes of different colors. If you can't find them, use any very ripe and tasty tomatoes. The sherry vinegar is the key to gazpacho, so seek out a heady one from Jerez in Spain—it will make all the difference.

To peel the tomatoes, fill a small bowl with ice and water and set aside. Bring a medium-sized saucepan of water to a boil. Using a sharp knife, score a cross in the top of each tomato. Drop the tomatoes into the hot water for just 30 seconds. Remove with a slotted spoon and drop into the ice water for 1 minute. Remove from the water and peel. Cut the tomatoes in halves or quarters, depending on the size, and put in the food processor.

Roughly chop the garlic, onion, and cucumbers then add to the tomatoes. Cut the green bell pepper and Serrano chile in half and remove all of the white pith and seeds. Chop both and add to the tomatoes. Pulse the mixture until it is chunky. Pour the gazpacho into a large bowl and stir in the olive oil and vinegar. Chill in the refrigerator until ready to serve.

Preheat the oven to 400°F.

To make the Smoked Salted Toasts, slice the baguette lengthwise into 4 and lay the slices on a baking sheet. Mix the garlic and olive oil in a small bowl and drizzle over the bread. Sprinkle with the smoked sea salt and bake in the preheated oven for 8–10 minutes until golden.

Pour the gazpacho into 4 bowls, season with the sea salt flakes and cracked black pepper, drizzle each bowl with a little olive oil and garnish with a few chives, if liked. Serve each bowl with a Smoked Salted Toast on the side.

chickpea, tomato, and green bean minestrone

2 tablespoons olive oil

1 onion, chopped

2 garlic cloves, chopped

14-oz. can chickpeas, rinsed and drained

4 oz. green beans, sliced on the angle

6 ripe tomatoes, halved

1 handful of chopped fresh flat leaf parsley

6 cups vegetable stock

4 oz. spaghetti, broken into short lengths

2 handfuls of arugula

½ cup finely grated aged pecorino or Parmesan, finely grated

sea salt and freshly ground black pepper

crusty bread, to serve

SERVES 4

Minestrone can be a hotchpotch of whatever takes your fancy. Often thought of as cold weather fare, this version has summer written all over it and is packed with fresh tomatoes and green beans as well as chickpeas, a pantry staple you should never be without. A few handfuls of arugula make a nice addition, as its peppery bite and fresh taste lightens the soup making it an ideal appetizer.

Put the oil in a large saucepan set over medium heat. Add the onion, partially cover with a lid, and cook for 4–5 minutes, stirring often, until softened. Add the garlic and cook for 1 minute. Add the chickpeas, green beans, tomatoes, parsley, stock, and spaghetti and bring to a boil.

Reduce the heat and let simmer, uncovered, for about 15–20 minutes, stirring often, until the spaghetti is cooked and the soup has thickened. Season to taste with salt and pepper.

Just before serving, add the arugula and gently stir until the arugula wilts and softens. Ladle into warmed serving bowls and sprinkle a generous amount of grated cheese over the top. Serve immediately with chunks of crusty bread on the side.

crab bisque

1½ lbs. whole cooked crab or
8 oz. lump crabmeat

5 cups fish stock

½ cup white wine

3 tablespoons unsalted butter

3 leeks, sliced

10 oz. potatoes, peeled
and diced

1 teaspoon tomato paste

3 tablespoons brandy

2 fresh tarragon sprigs

3 tablespoons heavy cream

¼ teaspoon ground mace

freshly squeezed juice of
½ a lemon

sea salt

a pinch of cayenne pepper,
to serve

crusty bread, to serve

SERVES 4

This impressive soup is very easy to make and is reminiscent of those rust-hued Mediterranean soups which taste of shellfish and have a hint of chile in them. For convenience, buy fresh, prepared crabmeat which comes in its shell.

Prise out the white and brown crabmeat from its shell, place in a small bowl and reserve. You should have at least 8 oz. meat. Put the shell, stock, and wine in a saucepan and simmer for 20 minutes.

Heat the butter in a large skillet set over low heat, then add the leeks. Cover and cook for 5 minutes until softened, but not browned. Add the potatoes and stir well, then replace the lid and cook for a further 5 minutes, stirring occasionally to stop it from sticking. Add the tomato paste, brandy, and tarragon and turn up the heat to burn off the alcohol. Once it has evaporated, strain in half the stock mixture and simmer until the potatoes are completely soft, about 15 minutes.

Transfer the contents of the skillet to a blender and liquidize until smooth. Return to the pan, strain in the remaining stock, then add the reserved crabmeat and the cream. Heat through and season to taste with salt, mace, and lemon juice.

Divide the soup between 4 serving bowls, sprinkle with a little cayenne pepper and serve with crusty bread on the side.

salads

double zucchini, parmesan, and walnut salad

3 tablespoons freshly squeezed lemon juice

finely grated peel of 2 lemons

½ teaspoon sea salt

6 tablespoons extra virgin olive oil

12 small (baby) zucchini

6 medium zucchini

½ cup walnuts, toasted

leaves from a small bunch of fresh basil or mint, chopped

2 oz. fresh Parmesan, shaved

freshly ground black pepper

a ridged stovetop grill pan

SERVES 6

This unusual and tasty salad is a combination of two styles of zucchini; larger ones marinated and pan-grilled for a deep flavor and soft texture, and baby zucchini very thinly sliced and marinated for a crunchy texture and fresh flavor.

To make the marinade, whisk together the lemon juice and peel with the salt and ¼ teaspoon black pepper in a small bowl, then slowly whisk in the oil.

Slice the small zucchini as thinly as possible, using a mandoline if you have one. Put in a shallow, non-reactive dish and pour over half the marinade. Cover and leave to marinate at room temperature for at least 1 hour and up to 6 hours, turning occasionally.

Thickly slice the medium zucchini and put them in another shallow, non-reactive dish. Pour over the remaining marinade, cover and leave to marinate at room temperature for 1 hour.

Heat a ridged stovetop grill pan until hot and pan-grill the medium zucchini for 1–2 minutes on each side. Let cool. Arrange both the marinated and grilled zucchini together on a serving dish and scatter over the walnuts and basil. Finish with shavings of Parmesan and freshly ground black pepper.

apple, beet, and fennel salad with roquefort

1 bunch of watercress, stems trimmed, leaves rinsed and dried

2 crisp green eating apples, halved, cored, and thinly sliced

1 fennel bulb, halved and thinly sliced

3 oz. Roquefort cheese, crumbled

a handful of fresh flat leaf parsley, finely chopped

a small bunch of chives, snipped

2 cooked beets

FOR THE VINAIGRETTE

2 tablespoons red or white wine vinegar

1 teaspoon fine sea salt

1 teaspoon Dijon mustard

7 tablespoons sunflower oil

1 tablespoon sour cream

freshly ground black pepper

SERVES 4

This is a colorful combination of crisp ingredients that makes a lively start to any meal. The mix of flavors and textures is very pleasing; if fennel is unavailable, you could substitute two celery ribs, thinly sliced.

First, prepare the vinaigrette. Put the vinegar in a bowl. Using a fork or a small whisk, stir in the salt until almost dissolved. Stir in the mustard. Stir in the oil, a tablespoon at a time, whisking well between each addition, until emulsified. Finally, stir in the sour cream and add pepper to taste.

Just before you're ready to serve the salad, tear the watercress into pieces and put it in a bowl with the apples, fennel, cheese, parsley, and chives. Pour over all but 2 tablespoons of the vinaigrette and toss gently with your hands.

Divide the salad between 4 serving plates and top each portion with some slices of beet. Drizzle the remaining vinaigrette over the top of each salad and serve immediately.

classic caesar salad

2 thick slices of dense
white bread

2 tablespoons olive oil

1 large romaine lettuce

2 oz. fresh Parmesan, grated
or shaved

CLASSIC CAESAR DRESSING

1 very fresh egg*, at room
temperature

1 small garlic clove, crushed

1 teaspoon Dijon mustard

1 teaspoon Worcestershire sauce

¼ teaspoon sea salt

⅛ teaspoon freshly ground
black pepper

1 tablespoon white wine vinegar

1 tablespoon freshly squeezed
lemon juice

4 tablespoons extra virgin
olive oil

4 anchovy fillets, finely chopped
(optional)

SERVES 4

This recipe is a rare perfection as it's true to the original classic Caesar salad. It makes a perfect appetizer as it's light yet full of flavor. To make a more substantial meal, just follow any of the additions listed below.

Cut the crusts off the bread and discard. Cut the bread into cubes. Heat the olive oil in a skillet, add the bread cubes and cook until golden brown. Set aside.

To make the Classic Caesar Dressing, put the egg in a small saucepan and cover with warm water. Bring to just simmering, turn off the heat and leave for 2 minutes. Run under cold water to stop the egg cooking any further.

Crack the egg into a large serving bowl and whisk in the garlic, mustard, Worcestershire sauce, salt, pepper, vinegar, and lemon juice. Slowly whisk in the extra virgin olive oil. Stir in the chopped anchovy fillets, if using. Add the lettuce to the bowl and toss well. Transfer to 4 serving plates then scatter over the Parmesan cheese and croûtons to serve.

Variations:

Chicken Caesar Roast 3–4 chicken breasts, preferably in a roasting bag to prevent them drying out, until golden and cooked through. Let cool then slice and add to the salad.

Bacon and avocado Caesar Fry 8 slices of bacon until crisp. Chop and add to the salad with 1 sliced avocado.

*Note This recipe uses partially cooked eggs. If you prefer to cook the eggs through, you can do this by increasing the cooking time to 6 minutes. Finely chop the egg before adding it to the dressing.

cherry tomato, bocconcini, and basil salad on bruschetta

4 tablespoons extra virgin olive oil

1 teaspoon balsamic vinegar

12 bocconcini, halved, or 13 oz. regular mozzarella cheese, cubed

20 ripe cherry tomatoes or pomodorini (baby plum tomatoes), halved

a handful of torn fresh basil leaves, plus extra to serve

1 cup arugula

sea salt and freshly ground black pepper

FOR THE BRUSCHETTA

4 thick slices country bread, preferably sourdough

2 garlic cloves, halved

extra virgin olive oil, for drizzling

SERVES 4

All the colors of the Italian flag are here in this delicious salad. This makes a great start to a rustic summer meal and the bruschetta is optional if you want an even lighter bite. *Bocconcini* (meaning "little bites") are tiny balls of mozzarella—they are the perfect size for this recipe but if you can't find them, use regular mozzarella cut into cubes.

Whisk 3 tablespoons of the olive oil with the balsamic vinegar. Season to taste with salt and pepper. Stir in the halved bocconcini or mozzarella cubes, tomatoes, and torn basil leaves. Set aside.

To make the bruschetta, broil, toast, or pan-grill the bread on both sides until lightly charred or toasted. Rub the top side of each slice with the cut garlic, then drizzle with olive oil.

Cover each slice of bruschetta with arugula and spoon over the tomatoes and mozzarella. Drizzle with the remaining olive oil and top with fresh basil leaves. Serve immediately as the bread will quickly become soggy.

meat and poultry

parma ham with figs and balsamic dressing

4 large fresh ripe figs (preferably purple ones)

1 tablespoon good balsamic vinegar

extra virgin olive oil, to drizzle

12 thin slices of Parma ham or prosciutto crudo

6 oz. fresh Parmesan, broken into rough chunks

extra virgin olive oil, to serve

cracked black pepper

SERVES 4

This is an all-time classic recipe. The combination of sweet, salty Parma ham and a soft, yielding ripe fig is one of life's little miracles. Choose a very good quality aged balsamic vinegar—it should be thick, sweet, and syrupy—and use it in tiny amounts. This is quick and easy to assemble, and best served at room temperature, rather than chilled, for maximum flavor.

Take each fig and stand it upright. Using a sharp knife, make 2 cuts across each fig not quite quartering it, but keeping it intact. Ease the figs open to form a "flower" and brush liberally with balsamic vinegar and olive oil.

Arrange 3 slices of Parma ham on each of 4 serving plates. Place a fig on top and scatter the Parmesan chunks over and around the fig. Drizzle with extra virgin olive oil and sprinkle with plenty of cracked black pepper. Serve at room temperature rather than chilled for maximum flavor.

chicken liver pâté
with blueberry and balsamic glaze

2 tablespoons olive oil

1 onion, finely chopped

2 garlic cloves, chopped

2 bay leaves

1 lb. chicken livers, cleaned and trimmed*

1 tablespoon ruby port

2 teaspoons soy sauce

¼ teaspoon ground nutmeg

¼ teaspoon ground cinnamon

½ teaspoon sea salt

¼ teaspoon freshly ground black pepper

fresh thyme, to garnish (optional)

grissini (Italian bread sticks), to serve

BLUEBERRY AND BALSAMIC GLAZE

1¼ cups fresh or frozen blueberries

3 tablespoons sugar

1½ teaspoons powdered gelatin

1 tablespoon balsamic vinegar

6 ramekins or small glass dishes

SERVES 6

This is a less rich, dairy-free alternative to traditional chicken liver pâté with a fruity berry glaze. It's a good choice as an appetizer as it's not too filling, especially when served with *grissini* instead of the more usual buttered toast.

To make the blueberry and balsamic glaze, put the blueberries, sugar, and ⅓ cup water in a saucepan. Bring to a boil, then continue to cook for 3 minutes. Strain through a fine strainer to give about ⅔ cup liquid. Sprinkle the powdered gelatin over the hot blueberry mixture and let soften for a few minutes. Add the balsamic vinegar and stir until the gelatin has dissolved. Leave to cool slightly before using.

Heat the olive oil in a large skillet set over medium heat. Add the onion, garlic, and bay leaves and sauté for 5 minutes, until the onion is translucent. Increase the heat, add the chicken livers and cook them, stirring, for 2–3 minutes until firm but still pink in the middle. Remove from the heat and discard the bay leaves. Spoon the chicken liver mixture into a food processor and add the port, soy sauce, nutmeg, cinnamon, salt, and pepper. Process in short bursts until you have a smooth pâté.

Spoon the pâté into 6 ramekins, level the tops and pour the blueberry glaze over the top. Leave to set then garnish with thyme, if using, and serve with grissini. This pâté will keep in the refrigerator for up to 3 days.

*Note To clean chicken livers, cut off any green specks of bile, pull away any sinew and connective tissue and discard, then rinse the livers.

seared steak carpaccio
with truffle vinaigrette and arugula

1¼ lbs. tenderloin*

2 tablespoons mixed peppercorns

1 teaspoon herbes de Provence

2 tablespoons olive oil

1 cup arugula

TRUFFLE VINAIGRETTE

2 tablespoons white wine vinegar

½ teaspoon balsamic vinegar

2 teaspoons white truffle-flavored olive oil

6 tablespoons light olive oil

2 tablespoons light cream

sea salt and freshly ground black pepper

shavings of fresh Parmesan, to serve

crusty bread, to serve (optional)

SERVES 6

Carpaccio is traditionally a raw steak dish, but in this version the meat is well seasoned and seared first. It makes an easy yet fabulously showy and colorful dinner party appetizer.

Trim the beef of any excess fat or sinew and pat dry with paper towels. Put the peppercorns in a mortar with the herbes de Provence and pound with a pestle until crushed. Coat all sides of the meat with the crushed peppercorns, wrap in plastic wrap and chill in the refrigerator for 1 hour.

Heat a skillet over medium to high heat for about 3 minutes until hot. Add the oil, heat for 1 minute, then brown the meat on all sides for 2–3 minutes, turning regularly to prevent the peppercorns burning. Set aside to cool, then rewrap the meat and put it in the freezer for about 45 minutes until firm.

To make the vinaigrette, put the vinegars in a bowl and season with salt and pepper. Whisk in the oils until the dressing is thick, then gradually add the cream. Taste and adjust the seasoning and set aside.

Slice the beef as thinly as you can with a very sharp knife and lay it between sheets of greaseproof paper. Beat it out with a meat mallet or rolling pin to make it thinner still.

Arrange the arugula on each of 4 serving plates, then lay over the slices of carpaccio. Spoon a little dressing over each portion. Top with shavings of Parmesan and serve with crusty bread, if liked.

*Note It's important to buy a piece of meat of an even thickness so that it cooks evenly.

pork and hazelnut rillettes

with pickled cucumbers

2¼ lbs. very fatty pork butt

7 fresh thyme sprigs

2 large garlic cloves, peeled

1 bay leaf

1 teaspoon sea salt

½ teaspoon freshly ground black pepper

½ cup white wine

½ cup whole blanched hazelnuts

toasted bread, to serve

PICKLED CUCUMBERS

6-inch length of cucumber

½ cup rice vinegar

½ cup sugar

6 individual serving pots or ramekins, each 4 oz. capacity

SERVES 6

A traditional means of preserving meat in fat, rillettes are a deliciously simple alternative to a heartier terrine. The hazelnuts add a lovely flavor as well as a delicious crunch and the tartness of the pickled cucumbers is just right.

To make the pickled cucumbers, cut the cucumber in half lengthwise and scoop out the seeds. Cut the flesh into very thin strips.

Put the rice vinegar and sugar in a saucepan and bring to a boil, stirring until the sugar has dissolved. Boil for 3 minutes. Cool and pour over the cucumber. Cover and refrigerate until needed.

Cut the pork butt into small pieces and put in a small, heavy-based casserole dish. Add 1 thyme sprig (reserving the rest as a garnish), the garlic, bay leaf, salt, and pepper and pour over the wine. Cover and cook over low heat for 3 hours until the meat is very tender.

Preheat the oven to 325°F.

Spread the hazelnuts in an even layer on a baking sheet. Bake in the preheated oven for 20 minutes, stirring occasionally, until the nuts are just smelling toasted. Put them in a clean kitchen towel and rub vigorously until the skins come loose. Discard the skins and roughly chop the nuts.

Transfer the pork into a colander set over a large bowl or pitcher, reserving all the juices. Using 2 forks, tear the pork into fine strips, or process briefly in a food processor. Combine the meat with the toasted hazelnuts and pack into the pots. Spoon the fatty juices over the meat and finish with a thyme sprig to garnish. Once cool, keep refrigerated until ready to serve. The rillettes will keep in refrigerator for up to 3 days.

fish and seafood

salt-crusted citrus shrimp
with chili dipping sauce

finely grated peel and freshly
squeezed juice of 2 limes

4 lbs. coarse sea salt

1 lb. raw jumbo shrimp, unshelled

CHILI DIPPING SAUCE

2 red chiles, finely chopped

4 fresh kaffir lime leaves,
finely shredded

1 scallion, finely chopped

1 garlic clove, finely chopped

½ cup fish sauce

finely grated peel and freshly
squeezed juice of 2 limes

1 tablespoon rice wine vinegar

1 tablespoon brown sugar

1 tablespoon unsalted peanuts,
chopped

SERVES 4

This is a showstopper at any dinner party. Crack open the salt crust at the table and let your guests be dazzled by the heavenly aromas and the bright pink shells.

Preheat the oven to 475°F.

In a large bowl mix together the lime peel and juice, salt and 1 cup water. The mixture should be the consistency of wet sand. Spread a layer of the salt mixture in a baking dish and arrange the shrimp on top. Cover with the remaining salt mixture and pat well down, making sure the shrimp are completely covered and there are no gaps anywhere.

Bake in the preheated oven for 15 minutes. The salt should be slightly golden on top.

Whisk together all the Chili Dipping Sauce ingredients until the sugar has dissolved. Divide between 4 small bowls.

When the shrimp are ready, take them out of the oven and leave them to rest for 5 minutes. Using the back of a knife, crack open the crust and remove the top part. Serve at the table.

Let guests help themselves, peel their own shrimp, and dip in the chili sauce. Have a large empty bowl handy for the shells.

smoked mackerel and preserved lemon pâté

with harissa crushed tomatoes

8 oz. smoked mackerel
fillets, skinned

rind of 1 small preserved lemon*,
finely chopped

3 tablespoons finely chopped
fresh dill

8 oz. cream cheese, softened

crisply toasted flat breads,
to serve

**HARISSA CRUSHED
TOMATOES**

1 cup cherry tomatoes

1 tablespoon harissa
(Moroccan hot chili paste)

6–8 ramekins

SERVES 8

A wonderfully quick pâté to make using smoked mackerel or any other moist smoked fish, this makes a simple yet impressive and delicious start to a meal.

Remove the skin and any stray bones from the mackerel fillets, flake the flesh into a bowl and mix with the preserved lemon, dill, and cream cheese. Cover and refrigerate until ready to serve.

In a small serving bowl, combine the cherry tomatoes and harissa, crushing the tomatoes lightly with the back of a fork.

Divide the pâté between the ramekins and serve with the Harissa Crushed Tomatoes and crisply toasted flat breads.

*Note Preserved lemons are used extensively in North African cooking and are whole lemons packed in jars with salt. The interesting thing is that you eat only the rind, which contains the essential flavor of the lemon. They are available from larger stores and specialist retailers.

pickled salmon with fennel and cucumber salad

1 lb. salmon fillet, skinned and boned

3–4 shallots, thinly sliced

4 tablespoons chopped dill

1 fennel bulb, with fronds if possible

½ cucumber, halved lengthwise and seeded

freshly squeezed juice of 1 lemon

1 teaspoon wholegrain mustard

3 tablespoons olive oil, plus extra for drizzling

sea salt and freshly ground black pepper

PICKLING LIQUID

1 cup white or rice vinegar

2 teaspoons sea salt

¼ cup granulated sugar

finely grated peel of 1 lemon

SERVES 4

This is a light and refreshing appetizer. The fish is marinated for several days, so do prepare ahead. Serve with boiled and buttered new potatoes to make a more substantial meal.

To make the pickling liquid, combine the vinegar, ½ cup water, salt, sugar, and lemon peel in a saucepan and bring to a boil. Simmer for 3 minutes, then let cool.

Put the salmon fillet in a shallow, non-reactive container with the shallots and dill. Pour over the pickling liquid and cover tightly. Leave in the refrigerator for 2–3 days, turning the salmon once a day.

To assemble the salad, remove the salmon from the pickling liquid and slice it into thin strips. Arrange the salmon on 4 serving plates with a few of the pickled shallots.

Slice the fennel and cucumber very thinly, using a mandoline if you have one, and put in a bowl. Chop the green fennel fronds, if available, very finely and add 3 tablespoonfuls to the bowl.

In a small bowl, whisk together the lemon juice, mustard, and oil and season to taste with salt and pepper. Just before serving, toss the dressing through the fennel and cucumber salad and arrange a little on top of the salmon. Drizzle with extra oil to serve.

chili salt squid

14 oz. cleaned squid
(1 large tube)

2 tablespoons cornstarch

1 tablespoon all-purpose flour

½ teaspoon ground white pepper

½ teaspoon mild chili powder

3 teaspoons sea salt

1 large red chile, thinly sliced

a small handful of cilantro leaves, chopped

vegetable oil, for deep-frying

lemon or lime wedges, to serve

SERVES 4

This is a delicious appetizer that's perfect for sharing when served on a large platter. Fresh squid can seem a little daunting, but it really is superior to frozen. Serve it with plenty of lemon or lime wedges for squeezing and a nice thirst-quenching aperitif to counter the heat of the chile.

Cut the squid tube down one side so that it opens up. Use a sharp knife to trim and discard any internal membranes. Cut it lengthwise into 1-inch wide strips, then cut each strip in half. Combine the cornstarch, flour, pepper, chili powder, and salt in a large bowl. Half-fill a large saucepan with the vegetable oil, set over high heat and heat until the surface of the oil shimmers.

Toss half of the squid pieces in the flour mixture, quickly shaking off the excess, and add them to the oil. Cook for about 2 minutes, until deep golden. Remove with a slotted spoon and drain on paper towels. Repeat with the remaining squid. Add the chile slices to the oil and cook for just a few seconds.

Remove from the pan and drain on paper towels. Put the squid and chile on a serving platter and sprinkle with the cilantro. Serve while still warm with plenty of lemon wedges on the side for squeezing.

vegetarian

smoked mushroom pâté

6 oz. cream cheese
½ teaspoon sea salt
6 tablespoons fresh dill
5 tablespoons butter
crackers or toast, to serve

SMOKED MUSHROOMS
½ cup all-purpose flour
½ cup sugar
½ cup rice
¼ cup tea leaves
12 oz. flat mushrooms
½ cup olive oil

an aluminium foil roasting dish or wok
a large ramekin

SERVE 4–6

This delicious recipe showcases the wonderful flavors of the smoked mushrooms. If you can find pre-smoked mushrooms, by all means use them—you will need 10 oz. Otherwise, it is quite easy to smoke your own at home.

Preheat a barbecue or element.

To make the smoked mushrooms, mix together the flour, sugar, rice, and tea and spread over the bottom of the roasting dish or wok.

Put the mushrooms in a single layer on a metal rack. Place the rack on the roasting dish containing the tea-leaf mixture. Cover loosely with a large piece of aluminium foil and crimp the edges to the roasting dish securely so that no smoke escapes.

Place on the preheated barbecue or element and heat for 15 minutes. Remove from the heat and leave, covered, to cool. Put the cooled mushrooms in a container and cover with the olive oil. Refrigerate until needed.

Put the drained smoked mushrooms, cream cheese, and salt in a food processor and process in bursts until well combined. Add 4 tablespoons of the dill and fold through. Spoon the pâté into the ramekin and smooth over the top. Chop the remaining dill and scatter over the pâté.

Melt the butter in a small saucepan. Remove from the heat and let the milk solids settle at the bottom, then pour the clarified butter over the top of the pâté, taking care to pour in as few of the milk solids as possible. Serve with crackers or toast.

cheese and basil souffles

¾ cup whole milk

4–6 sprigs of fresh basil

4 large eggs (or 5 if your whites are unusually small)

2 tablespoons butter

2 tablespoons all-purpose flour

½ cup grated Gruyère or sharp cheddar, grated

3 tablespoons freshly grated Parmesan, plus extra to dust the soufflé dish

sea salt and freshly ground black pepper

a 6-inch soufflé dish, about 3½ inches high, or 4 individual ramekins, lightly buttered

SERVES 4

Soufflés are one of the most impressive dishes you can make for your guests. You can make this delicious version in individual ramekins, as shown here, if you prefer. Simply reduce the baking time to 20–25 minutes.

Put the milk in a saucepan, add the basil, and bring slowly to a boil. Turn the heat very low, simmer for 1 minute, then turn off the heat and leave the basil to infuse for about 20 minutes.

Meanwhile, separate the eggs carefully—put the whites in a large, clean grease-free bowl and set aside 3 of the yolks to add to the sauce.

Preheat the oven to 400°F.

Set a large, heavy-based saucepan over medium heat and add the butter. When melted, stir in the flour. Cook for a few seconds, then pour in the warm, basil-infused milk through a strainer. Whisk together until smooth, then cook over low heat until thick. Stir in the grated Gruyère and most of the Parmesan and set back over low heat until the cheese has melted. Leave to cool for 5 minutes. Stir in the 3 egg yolks one by one.

Sprinkle the inside of the buttered soufflé dish with a little Parmesan, shaking off any excess. Put the dish on a baking sheet.

Whisk the egg whites and a pinch of salt until holding their shape but not stiff. Take 2 tablespoons of the whites and fold into the cheese base, then carefully fold in the rest of the whites without overmixing. Tip the mixture into the prepared soufflé dish. Sprinkle with a little more Parmesan and bake in the preheated oven for 25–30 minutes until the soufflé is well risen and browned. (Don't open the oven door or your soufflé may collapse!) Serve immediately.

naked spinach and ricotta ravioli
with sage cream

2¼ lbs. fresh spinach, well washed and roughly chopped

9 oz. ricotta

5 egg yolks

1¼ cups finely grated Parmesan, plus extra to serve

1 cup all-purpose flour

1 tablespoon butter

12 fresh sage leaves

1 cup light cream

sea salt and freshly ground black pepper

a baking sheet lined with baking paper

SERVES 3–4

These little balls of spinach and ricotta are called "naked" ravioli, as they are missing the pasta wrapping that usually encloses the filling. They can be made a day in advance and chilled in the fridge until you are ready to cook them.

Bring a large saucepan of water to a boil. Add the spinach and cook for 5 minutes, until wilted and tender. Rinse with cold water and drain well.

Tip the cooked spinach into the center of a clean kitchen towel. (This process will stain the kitchen towel so use an old, threadbare one, rather than your best.) Roll the towel up to form a log and twist the ends away from each other to squeeze out as much liquid as possible. Put the spinach on a chopping board and chop finely. Transfer to a large bowl. Add the ricotta, egg yolks, and half of the Parmesan and season to taste with salt and pepper. Mix well to thoroughly combine.

Put the flour on a large plate. Using slightly wet hands, roll the spinach mixture into 12 walnut-size balls. Lightly roll each ball in the flour and put them on the prepared baking sheet.

Put the butter and sage in a small saucepan and set over medium heat. Cook until the sage leaves just sizzle. Add the cream and the remaining Parmesan and cook for about 10 minutes, until thickened, stirring often to prevent the cream from catching on the bottom of the pan.

Bring a large saucepan of lightly salted water to a boil. Carefully drop the balls into the boiling water and cook for just 1 minute, until they rise to the surface. Drain well and arrange 3 or 4 balls in each serving dish. Spoon over the warm sage cream, sprinkle with the extra Parmesan and grind over plenty of black pepper. Serve immediately.

fresh asparagus
with homemade hollandaise sauce

1 lb. fresh asparagus spears, trimmed

cracked black pepper

HOLLANDAISE SAUCE

1 stick plus 2 tablespoons unsalted butter

2 tablespoons white wine vinegar

1 shallot, finely chopped

a pinch of sea salt

2 egg yolks

SERVES 4

Hollandaise is a smooth emulsion of butter, vinegar, and eggs. Rich and velvety, this sauce is pure heaven when partnered with simply cooked asparagus, and makes an indulgent yet light start to any special occasion meal.

To make the hollandaise, melt the butter very gently in a small saucepan. Pour it into a small pitcher through a cheesecloth-lined tea strainer to remove any excess milk solids.

Put the vinegar, shallot, salt, and 1 tablespoon water in a small saucepan and heat gently until the liquid is almost totally evaporated, leaving only about 1 tablespoon. Remove from the heat and strain into a glass bowl.

Place the bowl over a saucepan of gently simmering water (do not let the bowl touch the water). Add the egg yolks and, using a balloon whisk, whisk the mixture for 2 minutes, or until pale and frothy. Remove from the heat.

Using a handheld electric mixer, whisk in the melted butter, pouring it in in a slow, steady stream. Continue whisking until the sauce becomes thick and velvety. Cover and keep warm.

Steam or boil the asparagus, as preferred and arrange on 4 serving plates. Spoon over the warm hollandaise, sprinkle with a little cracked black pepper and serve immediately.

index

conversion chart

Volume equivalents:

American	Metric	Imperial
6 tbsp butter	85 g	3 oz.
7 tbsp butter	100 g	3½ oz.
1 stick butter	115 g	4 oz.
1 teaspoon	5 ml	
1 tablespoon	15 ml	
¼ cup	60 ml	2 fl.oz.
⅓ cup	75 ml	2½ fl.oz.
½ cup	125 ml	4 fl.oz.
⅔ cup	150 ml	5 fl.oz. (¼ pint)
¾ cup	175 ml	6 fl.oz.
1 cup	250 ml	8 fl.oz.

Oven temperatures:

120°C/130°C	(250°F)	Gas ½
140°C	(275°F)	Gas 1
150°C	(300°F)	Gas 2
160°C/170°C	(325°F)	Gas 3
180°C	(350°F)	Gas 4
190°C	(375°F)	Gas 5
200°C	(400°F)	Gas 6
220°C	(425°F)	Gas 7

Weight equivalents:

Imperial	Metric
1 oz.	30 g
2 oz.	55 g
3 oz.	85 g
3½ oz.	100 g
4 oz.	115 g
5 oz.	140 g
6 oz.	175 g
8 oz. (½ lb.)	225 g
9 oz.	250 g
10 oz.	280 g
11½ oz.	325 g
12 oz.	350 g
13 oz.	375 g
14 oz.	400 g
15 oz.	425 g
16 oz. (1 lb.)	450 g

Measurements:

Inches	Cm
¼ inch	0.5 cm
½ inch	1 cm
¾ inch	1.5 cm
1 inch	2.5 cm
2 inches	5 cm
3 inches	7 cm
4 inches	10 cm
5 inches	12 cm
6 inches	15 cm
7 inches	18 cm
8 inches	20 cm
9 inches	23 cm
10 inches	25 cm
11 inches	28 cm
12 inches	30 cm